Dancing to the Beat

By Kathy White

Rigby PM Collection and PM Plus
Emerald Level 26

U.S. Edition © 2013 HMH Supplemental Publishers
10801 N. MoPac Expressway
Building #3
Austin, TX 78759
www.hmhsupplemental.com

Text © 2003 Cengage Learning Australia Pty Limited
Illustrations © 2003 Cengage Learning Australia Pty Limited
Originally published in Australia by Cengage Learning Australia

All rights reserved. No part of this work may be reproduced or transmitted in any form or by any means, electronic or mechanical, including photocopying or recording, or by any information storage and retrieval system, without the prior written permission of the copyright owner unless such copying is expressly permitted by federal copyright law. Requests for permission to make copies of any part of the work should be addressed to Houghton Mifflin Harcourt Publishing Company, Attn: Contracts, Copyrights, and Licensing, 9400 Southpark Center Loop, Orlando, Florida 32819.

9 10 11   1957   14
18647

Text: Kathy White
Printed in China by 1010 Printing International Ltd

Acknowledgments
Photographs by AAP Image, p. 16; Australian Picture Library/ Corbis, pp. 9 bottom, 12 bottom left/ Bettmann, pp. 11 top right, 12 top left/ A. Souders, p. 22 bottom left/ Alison Wright, p. 6 right/ Catherine Karnow, p. 13 bottom left/ Jack Fields, p. 5 bottom/ Jack Moebes, p. 12 top right/ James L. Amos, p. 13 top right/ Kevin Fleming, p. 10 right/ Michael St. Maur Sheil, p. 8 bottom left/ Owen Franken, p. 14; Coo-ee Historical Picture Library, pp. 7 top, 8 top, 8 bottom right, 23 top; Lindsay Edwards, cover, pp. 15, 17; Fotopress. nz, p. 7 bottom; Getty Images, p. 11 top left/ Photodisc, p. 11 bottom left/ Stone/ Christopher Arnesen, p. 4l; Newspix, p.4 right; Photoedit/ David Young-Wolff, p. 22 bottom right; Photolibrary.com, p. 13 bottom right/ Index Stock Imagery, pp. 5 top, 6 left/ José Fuste Raga, p. 10 left/ Retro D, p. 13 top left; Picture Source/ Terry Oakley, p. 18 top; Stock Photos/ Corbis Stock Market, p. 9 top; The Art Archive/ Musée Carnavalet Paris/ Dagli Orti, p. 11 bottom right; Kathy White, pp. 18 bottom, 19, 20, 21, 22, 23 bottom.

Dancing to the Beat
ISBN 978 0 75 784129 3

Contents

CHAPTER 1		**Why Do We Dance?**	4
CHAPTER 2		**Dancing Through Time**	10
CHAPTER 3		**Strictly Spanish: Flamenco!**	14
		Try It Yourself	15
CHAPTER 4		**Basically Ballet**	16
		Try It Yourself	17
CHAPTER 5		**Choreography**	18
		Ann Dewey, Dancer and Choreographer	18
CHAPTER 6		**The V8s Rev Up**	20
		Andrew, V8 Dancer	20
CHAPTER 7		**Training to Be a Dancer**	22
GLOSSARY			24
INDEX			25

CHAPTER 1

Why Do We Dance?

Dance is one of the oldest and most creative ways of communicating. People can dance **solo**, in pairs, and in groups. When people dance, they move their bodies to a rhythm or beat.

For thousands of years, people all over the world have danced. Dances celebrate important events as well as day-to-day life. Some dances tell stories, some communicate emotions, and others are for fun, fitness, or entertainment.

Nature and Survival

In the days before supermarkets and refrigerators, people grew their own food. When they planted their crops, they performed special dances to encourage the crops to grow well. After they picked the crops, they danced at harvest festivals to give thanks for their food. Some of these dances are still performed today.

Native American people performed rain dances in times of **drought**.

▼ Japanese dancers take part in Sakura festivals to celebrate the beginning of spring. Streets are lined with cherry trees in blossom — Japan's national flower.

Family Events

People dance at births, **funerals**, weddings, and **coming-of-age** celebrations. The dances are a way to tell stories and pass on traditions. They bring families closer together.

▼ At 13, a Jewish boy becomes an adult. Men and boys dance together at a traditional coming-of-age celebration called a bar mitzvah.

▲ In Tibet, a dancer in a special costume performs at a funeral.

◀ The haka

War and Peace

New Zealand Maori **warriors** used to perform a war dance before and after a battle. Dancing helped them to strengthen their muscles, practice their fighting techniques, and to fight as a team. The dance was called the haka.

The haka still survives today and is performed by the New Zealand rugby team before international competitions.

▼ The New Zealand rugby team

◀ Australian Aboriginal dancers

Religious Beliefs

Some dances are about religious beliefs. Australian Aboriginal dancers decorate their bodies in patterns with **ochre**. They perform their dance to make contact with the spirits, the land, and their ancestors.

History and Culture

Many countries around the world have their own special dances. Some dances are very old. They are an important way of keeping a country's history and **culture** alive.

A traditional dancer ▶ from Bali.

◀ Irish dancers dress in costumes decorated with traditional designs. Their **jigs** and music tell stories from Irish folklore and history.

Recreation

Dance is a very popular **pastime**. Some people dance for fun and to keep fit, while others dance in competitions. Many people take part, while others enjoy watching.

◀ **Aerobic** dancing is made up of movements that are designed to improve physical fitness.

▼ Ballroom dancers perform in competitions.

CHAPTER 2

Dancing Through Time

Some dances are performed the same way today as they were hundreds of years ago. Others have changed or been forgotten.

In the last 100 years, advances in technology have led to many new musical styles, such as jazz, blues, rock 'n' roll, pop, and rap. People had to invent new ways of moving to the music. Here are some of the dances.

550 BC
Spanish Dance

Some Spanish dances that are performed today can be traced back to ancient times.

Belly dancing came from a Middle Eastern folk dance.

500 AD
Belly Dance

1400s
Ballet

Ballet was first danced in the Italian royal court. In the 1600s, ballet became popular in France at the court of King Louis XIV.

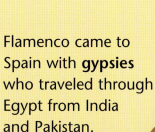

Flamenco came to Spain with **gypsies** who traveled through Egypt from India and Pakistan.

1700s
Flamenco
Waltz

Couples held each other closely as they danced the Waltz.

1800s

Barn Dance
Can-can
Tango
Tap Dance

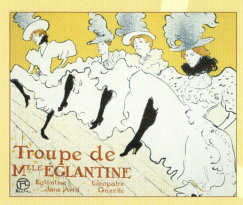

Nightclub dancers in Paris kicked their legs and waved their skirts high in the air when they danced the Can-can.

1910–1920s

Bunny Hug
Fox Trot
Grizzly Bear
Turkey Trot
Charleston

The Charleston was a popular dance craze of the 1920s.

1930s

Boogie-woogie
Cha-cha
Jitterbug
La Conga

> **TECHNOLOGY FACT**
> Dance crazes began soon after recorded music and radio were invented. The dances often had funny, descriptive names.

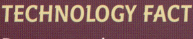

The Boogie-woogie and the Jitterbug were fast dances with lots of kicking and jumping.

1940s–1950s

Bop
Jive
Mambo
Rock 'n' Roll

Dancers performed energetic moves that suited the new rock 'n' roll music.

1960s
Mashed Potato
Jerk
Twist

People twisted their hips back and forth in the Twist.

1970s
Disco Dance

1980s
Break-dance
Rap-dance

TECHNOLOGY FACT
Colored, flashing lights were part of the disco scene. The new lighting effects helped set the mood.

Teenagers started Break-dancing on the streets of big cities. They held dance competitions.

1990s to today
Hip-hop
Macarena
Salsa
Street Funk
Dance Parties

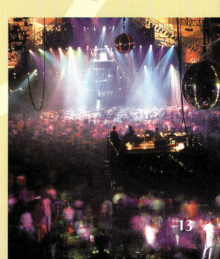

Dance parties are held at huge warehouses where thousands of people can dance.

CHAPTER 3

Strictly Spanish: Flamenco!

There are many kinds of Spanish dance. Flamenco dance developed in the southern region of Andalucia.

Flamenco dancers perform fast and complicated footwork that makes rhythmic sound patterns. Special dance shoes have metal studs in the soles and heels so that they make loud sounds.

Singing, guitar music, hand clapping, and dramatic costume and movement are all parts of flamenco dance.

▼ Today, flamenco dancers play castanets in some of their dances.

Try It Yourself!

Try these flamenco foot exercises on a wooden floor. Wear a pair of shoes with a hard sole and a strong heel.

> **Timing Tip:** Allow the same amount of time in between each stamp of the foot.

1 Lift your left foot. Stamp your heel on the floor, and lift your foot. ▶

2 Stamp the ball of your foot into the floor, and bring your heel down sharply behind it. Your left foot is now flat on the floor. ▼

3 Perform moves 1 to 2 with your right foot. ▶

Go back to the left foot and continue from one foot to the other. Move across the floor until you get faster and faster.

CHAPTER 4

Basically Ballet

A ballet performance can tell a story through dance. Ballet is made up of set steps, movements, and **positions**.

▼ A scene from *Swan Lake*.

TECHNOLOGY FACT
Today, advanced technology is used to create beautiful set designs and lighting effects. Lighting helps to set the mood for a ballet.

Ballet dancers need to be strong and **flexible**. Ballerinas dance on their toes, called *en pointe*. They have to train for many years before their feet and legs are strong enough.

The rules of ballet that girls and boys learn today are almost exactly the same as when they were first invented in France 400 years ago.

Try It Yourself!

There are five basic feet positions used in ballet. Try sliding your feet from one position to the next. You will need to turn out your legs from your hips.

Be Careful: Don't turn your legs out too far at first! It takes a lot of practice to become flexible enough to do these steps.

◀ **First position:** Turn your toes (and legs) out to the side with your heels touching.

Second position: Slide one ▶ foot out to the side and put it flat on the floor.

◀ **Third position:** Cross one foot halfway in front of the other, keeping your toes (and legs) pointing out.

Fourth position: Place the ▶ front foot exactly in front of the other with a space between them.

◀ **Fifth position:** Move the front foot back so that it is firmly pressed up against the other foot. Your feet and legs should still be turned out.

CHAPTER 5

Choreography

A lot of planning goes into a dance performance. The **choreographer** makes up the steps and movements that the dancers will perform. The routine, or plan, of steps is called the choreography.

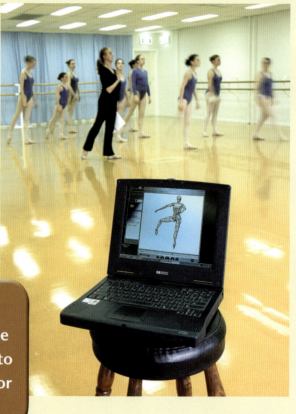

TECHNOLOGY FACT

Choreographers can use the latest computer programs to design the choreography for a dance performance.

Ann Dewey, Dancer and Choreographer

Ann Dewey started ballet dancing when she was three years old. As she got older, she tried all sorts of dance. When she was seventeen, Ann went to study **contemporary** dance in London.

Interview

ANN: *I like choreography because it is very creative. When I plan a dance, I come up with movement ideas, and make notes. Then I do **workshops** with other people. We usually try the steps in many different ways.*

One of Ann's dance workshops

TECHNOLOGY FACT
Ann learned how to write down choreography, but now she records it using a video camera.

Most of the time, I don't picture a dance in my head. I have to try it out and see what it looks like. Dance is a very **visual** art form.

Sometimes I try to tell a story through dance. Other times the dance is about creating shapes and patterns. There are no rules. A dance doesn't have to have a beginning, middle, and end. I could create a whole dance about creeping or jumping.

CHAPTER 6

The V8s Rev Up

The V8s are cheerleaders for a women's basketball team. Their routines are a mix of hip-hop steps and sports skills.

The V8s live far away from each other, but this weekend, they are together for two busy days of **rehearsals**.

TECHNOLOGY FACT

The V8s learn their moves by watching videos of their team-mate and choreographer, Gandalf, who runs through the new routines.

In two weeks' time, the V8s will be in the sports stadium ready to perform!

Andrew,
V8 Dancer

The dancers in the V8s had to **audition** for the job. Andrew was one of 100 people who auditioned.

Interview

ANDREW: *On the day of the auditions, we were taught some exercises and dance routines to perform in front of the judges. We also had 60 seconds to do something of our own. People sang, juggled, did some rap ... all sorts of things.*

The judges were looking for more than just good dance skills. They wanted people who looked like they were having fun when they danced.

The judges chose eight of us. We are all fit and like sports, but not everyone has had dance training. I'm an experienced dancer, but dancing isn't my full-time job. It's my hobby.

Andrew has done ballroom and Latin-American dancing, as well as hip-hop and street funk.

Gandalf is a **professional** dancer.

CHAPTER 7

Training to Be a Dancer

If you've decided that you would like to be a dancer one day, here are some useful tips.

1. Ask your family for encouragement and support.

2. Try many different dance classes, such as ballet, modern, and tap. After a while you may prefer one style of dance.

▶ Modern

▲ Ballet

Tap ▶

3. Talk to any friends who dance. They can help you find the best dance teachers.

4. Take part in as many performances as you can, at school and at your dance studio. This will give you experience in dancing in front of an audience.

5. When you are in high school, you should explore the dance programs available at colleges, universities, and fine art schools. Find out what **qualifications** you need for the school you like, and work hard to achieve them.

Good luck!

▶ Sarah has nearly finished training to be a professional dancer. Soon she will audition for her first dance job.

Glossary

aerobic	makes us breathe in lots of air
audition	to test performers to find the best dancer for the job
choreographer	person who makes up the plan of steps in a dance
coming-of-age	becoming an adult
contemporary	modern, up-to-date
culture	a traditional way of life of a group of people
drought	a long time without rain
flexible	able to move and bend easily
funeral	a ceremony that takes place soon after someone dies
gypsies	people who travel around, with no fixed home
jigs	lively, energetic dances
ochre	a colored clay used as yellow, brown, or red paint
pastime	a hobby
positions	special poses in ballet
professional	being paid to do a particular type of job
qualification	knowledge or skill needed
rehearsals	practice performances
solo	alone
visual	to do with using your eyes
warriors	people who are experienced fighters
workshops	classes where dancers try out new dance moves